BE THE ONE TO HEAL YOUR SELF: A WORKBOOK FOR PEOPLE WHO WANT RESULTS NOW

Written by Beth Rogerson, PhD
Produced by Moondog Marketing & Media in Stockholm, Sweden.

First Publication Date: October 2016

Table of Contents

Preface iii

Introduction vi

Note on Sources and Further Reading xi

Chapter One: Meet Your Protectors 1

Chapter Two: Getting to Know Your Bodyguards 16

Chapter Three: Discovering Your Exiles 32

Chapter Four: Moving Forward 54

Chapter Five: Rescue Chapter 72

Conclusion 78

Acknowledgments 80

PREFACE

When I wrote my first book *Inner Harmony: Putting Your Self Back in Charge,* I only knew that I was driven by the desire to bring the Internal Family Systems (IFS) approach to self-understanding to more people.

About five years ago I started to notice a part was up in me. This part was frustrated that I could only see one person or couple at a time for a counseling session in my office. I knew that IFS could do a lot of good for a lot of people - if only they knew about it.

I noticed too that at that time all of the materials available about IFS were written *by* IFS therapists, *for* IFS therapists. There was nothing written for the layman. Nothing easy to digest for people like my clients who could benefit from using an IFS approach to bringing balance and harmony to their own lives.

I firmly believe you don't need an advanced degree to eliminate depression, anxiety, burnout, or just feeling low in general.

I wrote *Inner Harmony* to put the IFS tools into your own hands. In the book I refer to it as "IFS goggles." Put them on, look at your inner world, and discover:

- All of the different parts who work together to get things done and to protect you from bad feelings

- Self, the core being of you that holds the qualities of Calm, Compassion, Curiosity, Creativity, Clarity, Courage, Connection, and Confidence

From there, the book begins to show you how to use the first three qualities of Self to begin to restore and rebalance your life.

Why Write About Your Parts?

The inspiration for this workbook you're holding right now came from a client who remarked he was struggling to get to know his inner world of parts without a lot of noise and interruptions. What steps could he take to get to know his parts before they got extreme?

Many people struggle to go inside of themselves to get to know their world of different parts. *Be the One to Heal Your Self: A Workbook for People Who Want Results Now* builds on *Inner Harmony* and takes it deeper.

I think you'll find this workbook especially helpful if you're someone who wants to:

- Feel calmer on the inside and in your life

- Lift those feelings of depression, anxiety, or worthlessness and feel better

- Stop beating yourself up for making mistakes or daring to dream big

- Change personal habits that have become too much such as drinking, shopping, or watching TV and instead make choices that fit your life better

- Enjoy life and the people around you more

This book will help you:

- Meet your unique inner protective system, so you can begin to heal

- Begin to connect to yourself better from the inside out

- And as a result, connect better on the outside of you too!

At times it may feel just like a family reunion when you go inside and look around: the fun of reconnecting, the awkwardness of meeting new people, the hesitation to talk to the black sheep in the family.

At times getting to know yourself from the inside out may feel hard. You'll meet parts of you who carry old wounds or traumas, and you'll feel some of those feelings all over again.

But take heart. This book will make it easier to get to know all of these parts inside you. Why not get to know them? They are there no matter what. Because this book gives you the framework to meet you parts in Self, you'll find you're more fully seated in Self leadership in your life.

I believe you're worth the effort. I hope you do, too.

INTRODUCTION

> "And you? When will you
> begin that long journey into yourself?"
>
> — Rumi

A wound is a wound is a wound.

In my 25 years of clinical practice, I've met many people who believed they shouldn't feel depressed or anxious because "nothing bad had ever happened" to them. And yet they did feel that way. That's why they were in my office.

Too often, we think trauma only comes from catastrophic events or tragedies like sexual violation, war, or physical abuse.

But even small events can leave us with wounds that, over time, cause trouble for us. To help clarify, I'll share an origin story that helped in the creation of one of my parts.

Many years ago as a young child, I was at a family reunion where we had all made real ice cream! It was finally time to eat it. We all stood in a line in front of my uncle as he carefully spooned this homemade frozen delight into each child's bowl.

Soon it was my turn for my bowl to be filled. My eyes were wide and my mouth was watering as I stood with my bowl outstretched. Just then, my uncle, without noticing me, said "I think everyone has gotten some ice cream now," and he took a big spoonful and put it into his mouth.

What about me? Didn't he see me? I didn't know it at the time, but a part was born right then. This young part of me formed a belief: *I have to jump in and go first, or else nobody will remember to take care of me.*

This belief grew stronger each time I found myself in other childhood situations where I was not seen and, indirectly, not cared for.

When this story came back to me, I realized this younger part had suffered real emotional pain each time it felt forgotten and overlooked. To protect myself from those feelings, another part was formed that made sure *I always rushed to be first in group situations.* I finally knew why.

~

The Internal Family Systems (IFS) framework for self understanding reveals that each of us have a protective system of competing sub-personalities. Those are the **parts**. You've been hearing from them your whole life, but you probably have never really met them.

You'll notice that there's not just one voice. There are many different voices and personalities in there. There's one part that's afraid of change, another part that's happy, another part that's sad and so forth.

It's important to remember **there are no bad parts of you**. They all have good intentions for you, even the troublesome ones. (I recommend reading my other book, *Inner Harmony*, if you're interested in learning more about understanding the motivations of your extreme parts.)

Fortunately, there's something else inside you besides all of these very noisy parts. You have **Self**. Self is your core being. You'll know Self is in charge - and not a noisy part - because you'll feel the eight qualities of Self:

- Calm

- Compassion

- Curiosity

- Courage

- Creativity

- Connection

- Confidence

- Clarity

The way to calm the inner noise and restore yourself to harmony is to start journaling. *Be the One to Heal Your Self: A Workbook for People Who Want Results Now* can help you open the lines of communication between you and your emotional or extreme parts. Beginning a dialogue creates a connection so your Self qualities of Calm, Curiosity, and Compassion can flow back and forth.

Journaling will continue to help you unfold the roots of some extreme behavior that is causing problems for you. You will find empathy for the parts that manage your worries or fears in ways that control or hurt yourself or others.

How to Use This Book

I strongly recommend starting with Chapter One and going in order from there, with the exception being Chapter Five, the rescue chapter. At any point while you are working through this book and you start to feel like you're in emotional crisis, you can skip to Chapter Five to help you cope with feeling too overwhelmed, sad, angry, hurt, frustrated, or vulnerable. You can use this chapter over and over again, if you need to.

In Chapter One, you'll get the lay of the land so to speak. You'll get introduced to many of your parts and start to understand them and their needs. These parts work hard to take care of you! But when they're working too hard (we call this being extreme or triggered), they can lead to you feeling stressed out, exhausted, unbalanced, anxious, and/or depressed.

In Chapter Two, you'll go deeper. What are these protecting parts working so hard to protect you from? If you have a part that always rushes to be first, you'll have the opportunity to hear from that part about what happens that makes it push so hard. The exercises will guide you in using your Self qualities to help these inner protectors begin to relax. That will ease some stress and exhaustion in your inner system, but to really overcome those feelings you'll need to get to the root of the issue.

Chapter Three is the toughest one, because you'll meet your exiled parts. These younger parts of you hold a lot of emotional pain because of the negative and difficult experiences they had. From these experiences, they developed painful beliefs. In the past you may have tried to meet them and had little success. It will be different this time because these exercises will provide the support and structure you need to feel safe inside as you meet them. As you bring Calm, Compassionate caring to these younger parts, you'll begin to heal from the inside out.

Chapter Four is about the future. You've set the stage for a new beginning. How will things be different inside for you, and how will that affect your outside world too? The possibilities are (excitingly) endless.

Before You Get Started: Get to Know the Eight Qualities of Self

We are more than just our parts. Self is a necessary ingredient of a fully functioning inner system. Self brings all of our parts into harmony. The IFS lens helps us fully understand Self by describing it as eight qualities.

When you recognize those qualities in yourself, that's how you know your greater Self is present. To put it another way, you're not blended and leading from an extreme part of yourself.

I go into more detail about Self in *Inner Harmony* but here's what you need to know to get started with this workbook.

- **Calm:** This is serenity. A smooth ocean where you sense a spaciousness and evenness.

- **Compassion:** Compassion is shared suffering. You feel someone else's pain and you feel caring concern for them. In this case, you will give Compassion to your parts. You might say, "I am so sorry this is so hard for you right now."

- **Curiosity:** This is nonjudgmental, open wondering. You might say toward a part of you, "Tell me more...How is it for you?"

- **Courage:** A feeling of awe and excitement. Feeling scared and moving toward this activity or event.

- **Creativity:** Being playful and imaginative. When you are creative you perceive the world in new ways and find hidden possibilities.

- **Connection:** An aliveness and a knowing between two or more people or parts. A reciprocity and flow of ideas and energy, a union and link.

- **Confidence:** A deep knowing. A connection to an inner truth.

- **Clarity:** Clearly knowing the answer despite the difficulties. In Clarity you do not feel confusion.

NOTE ON SOURCES AND FURTHER READING

Richard C. Schwartz, PhD, is the creator of IFS therapy and founder of the Center for Self Leadership. I am a student and practitioner of this model.

The subject matter of this book and the exercises here are drawn from Richard's work and a variety of other sources, which I list here. I have adapted them as I have evolved my own technique.

Internal Family Systems Reading

Introduction to the Internal Family Systems Model
Richard C. Schwartz PhD (2001)

Self-Therapy: A Step-by-Step Guide to Creating Wholeness, and Healing Your Inner Child, Using Internal Family Systems (IFS), A Cutting-Edge Psychotherapy
Jay Earley, PhD (2010)

Intimacy from the Inside Out: Courage and Compassion in Couple Therapy
Toni Herbine-Blank MS, RN, Cs-P, Donna M. Kerpelman JD, MS, and Martha Sweezy, PhD (2015)

Parts Work: An Illustrated Guide to Your Inner Life
Tom Holmes, PhD (2011)

Parts Psychology: A Trauma-Based, Self-State Therapy for Emotional Healing
Jay Noricks, PhD (2011)

Inner Harmony: Putting Your Self Back in Charge
Beth Rogerson, PhD (2015)

Healing from Trauma Reading

The Body Keeps the Score: Brain, Mind, and Body in the Healing of Trauma
Bessel A. van der Kolk (2014)

iRest Program For Healing PTSD: A Proven-Effective Approach to Using Yoga Nidra Meditation and Deep Relaxation Techniques to Overcome Trauma
Richard C. Miller (Author), Audrey Schoomaker (Introduction) (2015)

Self Compassion
Kristin Neff, PhD (2011)

Anger: Buddhist Wisdom for Cooling the Flames
Thich Nhat Hanh (2001)

The Fear Cure: Cultivating Courage as Medicine for the Body, Mind, and Soul
Lissa Rankin, MD (2015)

Yoga for Depression: A Compassionate Guide to Relieve Suffering Through Yoga
Amy Weintraub (2003)

MEET YOUR PROTECTORS

"Meet the little voices inside your head."
— tagline for Pixar's *Inside Out*

Those little voices, as *Inside Out* calls them, come from your **parts**. You've been hearing from your parts your whole life, but have you met them? Probably not. In this chapter you are going to get acquainted with your parts.

Getting to know your parts begins with **noticing** them when they're speaking to you. It's the first step toward inner harmony.

In Chapter One, the focus is on getting to know your **protector parts** so that you can meet your exiled parts later. It's important to ground yourself in your protectors before meeting your exiles.

Your protectors that are managers are those parts of you that run your life on a day-to-day basis. When they're in healthy roles, they help balance your life. When they become extreme, they hijack your system and can leave you feeling depressed, anxious, unbalanced, angry, sad, unhappy, or worse.

It's important to remember all of your parts have good intentions for you. This is true even for what seem to be your most troublesome parts. They're coping mechanisms developed to protect you from when you were very young.

They helped you many times throughout your life. The goal is *not* to get rid of any of your parts. Besides, you can't get rid of any parts because they are a part of you!

The goal *is* to guide extreme parts back into healthy roles by getting to know them and their roles in protecting you better. When these parts feel connected to your Self qualities, they can be transformed so that they don't have to be extreme in order to help you.

If your parts become extreme, or your younger, more vulnerable parts come up for you during this chapter, I recommend going right to Chapter Five for a rescue exercise.

Then, when you're ready, resume your work here.

With Self in charge, you can connect to your different parts and get to know them from a caring, nonjudgmental place. This connection gives you a way to be with and then release the emotional pain that's been hidden deep inside you. Once the pain is gone there's nothing to protect. Your protector parts can relax or find a new role, and you'll feel calmer on the inside.

Exercise One: Ice-breaker with shapes, colors & words (the living room exercise)

When you're meeting new people, an ice-breaker exercise is just the ticket to helping people relax. This exercise taps into your natural Self quality of Creativity to get to know the usual suspects - the parts who hang out the most in the living room of your mind.

You're going to sketch out your usual suspects using shapes, colors, and words. If you have markers or crayons, go get them! Otherwise, a pen or pencil will do just fine.

Directions

Draw stick figures, shapes, colors, and words to illustrate your parts.

Is there a planning part who always makes sure you stay organized and on schedule, or an angry part who takes over when they believe someone is taking advantage of you?

Where are they located in your living room of your mind? What words do you associate with these parts? What are their characteristics? You don't need to be a master at drawing. You could draw a face and write CRITIC on it. Or maybe a nickname like DRILL SERGEANT.

Write down any insights you have as you draw your parts. No need to get into lots of detail - you can save that for Exercise Two.

Exercise Two: A meeting of the minds

Look at your answers from Exercise One. Now you have a list of your regulars and it's time to learn more.

Directions

Discover what makes these parts tick by answering the following questions. You want to answer this question for each part you met in Exercise One.

What is this part's name? Or what would this part want to call itself?

How does this part make you feel when it's triggered?

Do you sense this part in a certain part of your body? What does it feel like?

Does this part have relationships with any of your other parts? What are these other parts and how do they influence each other or get along?

What more did you learn about this part? Can you describe its personality?

What does it see its purpose or job is for you? How does it see that it helps you?

Thank your part for coming out to meet you before turning to the next one and asking those questions. You can use blank pages at the back of the book to write more.

Exercise Three: Finding friends and foes

Surprise: your internal family members probably do not all get along! Some parts will actually shun, not listen to, or even try to get rid of other parts.

When you did Exercises One and Two, you may have met parts you sensed you didn't like. Maybe you sensed another part of you that felt like "all this part ever does is cause me trouble." If you've never considered the *positive* intention of this troublesome part, you may agree with your other parts: this troublesome part has got to go!

Except, there's no getting rid of parts. But it is possible to heal them with Self energy.

Directions

It's drawing time again. Now that you have sketched out the parts in your living room, gotten to know each part a little bit more, and identified any enemies or alliances, draw your living room again incorporating this new information.

In this exercise you will learn what kind of relationships your parts have to each other.

For example I found out my tired part often hangs out with my sad feelings. Not always but sometimes. Often people find they have a hater part. One that hates the perfect part or procrastinator.

How do they look and feel? What are they up to - taking center stage, sitting behind the curtains, sleeping in the corner?

Use this space to visualize how your parts relate to each other. Use shapes, stick figures, words or colors to identify your parts and their characteristics. Make notes about any insight you glean from this exercise.

Exercise Four: Opening the lines of communication at the Meeting Place

This exercise will help you improve the relationships between your parts. When parts understand each other, and maybe even see how they agree on some things, they can get along better and not cause so much trouble inside. The way to open the lines of communication is to be there with them and the eight qualities of Self (Calm, Compassion, Curiosity, Courage, Creativity, Connection, Confidence, Clarity). There will be deeper listening and understanding.

This exercise is more of a meditation than the others. After, you'll want to journal any insights you gained at the Meeting Place.

Directions

Decide where it would be comfortable and safe to have a meeting of your internal parts. Then, relax and go inside to hold the meeting. Bring your adult Self to this meeting. Name the issue you'd like to discuss.

Invite any parts that have ideas or opinions about this issue to come to the Meeting Place. Two polarized parts or more could show up at the meeting place. Take a look around and describe what parts of you have shown up: what do you observe, sense, feel, imagine?

Let your parts know that you want to hear each one around this issue - one at a time. If your parts start interrupting each other, kindly remind them to step back and listen. If they cannot do this then excuse yourself from the target part and move to the highly charged part of yourself and agree to come back and listen to the other one later.

Extend Curiosity, Calm, and Compassion toward your parts at the meeting by letting them know you are Curious to listen and find out what they all have to share. Ask who wants to go first and then wait and see what you notice, feel, and think. That is the part that will go first.

As you listen to this part, notice if you feel open and welcoming. Extend your Curiosity with no agenda - you are just being and listening. Encourage it to tell you more.

See how you feel towards this part and check to make sure you have not become blended with a helping part or a controlling part. If you feel Curious towards it and ready to listen there is a good chance you are not trying to control or "help" it decide what to do.

Breathe in Calm to your body by taking several deep breaths. Feel the calm and imagine spaciousness inside of you.

Now be with this part and hear its worries, concerns, and what it hopes for.Make some notes if you want.

If any part of you tries to interrupt, let them know you will listen to them just like this when it is their turn to talk. Ask them all to listen too.

When the part is finished ask this part, Are you finished / is there more?

After listening to this first part, let it know you heard it and value its input. Now step back into your Self after listening by breathing deeply into your lungs. Feel the Calm that comes into your body. Breathe in more Calm and hold all that you have just experienced simultaneously.

See if there is another part that wants to talk uninterrupted while you and any other parts listen.

After all the parts have shared how they see this issue and their fears and concerns, see if there are two parts that want to talk and listen with each other. Do this now or make arrangements to do this at a later time.

Notice yourself in Self energy, extending Calm and Curiosity towards your parts. Ask them to talk one at a time and one listen without interrupting. Then switch.

Observe in Self energy, encouraging your parts to take turns talking and listening.

Give the listening part the chance to speak and repeat the steps.

In closing, see if anyone would like to say something before ending. Thank all parts for their participation even ones that only watched or listened. Ask the parts if they can find a place where they will be comfortable until the next meeting.

See if there is a part of you that would like to share anything they heard that was new or different as a result of this meeting. What would Self say, after having listened to everything?

Coming from the place of Self, journal your thoughts and insights about what you are experiencing in your body right now.

CHAPTER TWO

GETING TO KNOW
YOUR BODYGUARDS

"Anger is just Sad's bodyguard."

— Lisa Palmer

In this chapter, you're going to:

- Get to know the parts you met in Chapter One

- Learn what they see their role is for you in your life

- Understand how they interact with other parts inside of you

These parts make up an interacting system inside of you.

These are your protector parts. Your protectors are the daily managers and firefighters who show up in your life to protect you from upsetting emotions. Your protectors are always motivated by a desire to protect you from being hurt, upset, or sad.

In other words, they're your bodyguards.

- **Managers** believe in prevention. Their role is to prevent bad feelings from happening. It doesn't matter whether the bad feelings come from your exiled parts, other extreme parts, or other people in your external world. Your manager parts are there to keep you safe.

- **Firefighters** do damage control. When exiled parts wreak havoc inside, your firefighters rush in to put out the fire by engaging in behaviors like excessive eating, shopping, or channel surfing. They may even engage in more immediately destructive behaviors like self harm and substance abuse.

As I described in Chapter One, managers can get extreme in your life and make living hard, and firefighters can make bad decisions for us because they're in reactive mode.

It would be better to shift into Self than into a part when making decisions.

You can get better at shifting into Self by getting to know your protectors better so you can identify when you are reacting from one of these parts.

Exercise One: A game of 20 questions

Like I mentioned, your protectors have nothing but good intentions for you. Even if they seem difficult or destructive at times. Your protectors are coping mechanisms you developed to protect you from shame, fear, sadness, and so on.

These parts of you are still working hard to keep you sheltered from uncomfortable feelings, memories, and emotional triggers. This exercise will help you get to know and understand the motivations behind their actions - to find out what their good intentions are.

There are many different ways to get to know your parts. Most of the time we just think about them and try to analyze them. I like the 20 questions exercise because the structure of it allows you to really hear from your part.
In turn, your part will feel listened to by Self, which builds trust and connection in your inner family system.

Directions

This exercise gives this part a guided opportunity to be listened to by your larger Self. Identify one of your loudest parts and get their perspective by asking them these questions.

By giving this part a guided opportunity to be listened to by your larger Self, you are opening up inside to the possibilities of feeling those Self qualities and giving them a chance to know Self - which creates trust in your overall system.

If another part tries to interrupt, ask that part to let the other finish and to wait its turn. Remember, this is (just) a part of you. So these answers are information from that part, *not* all of you.

1. If you could only hear one song for the rest of your life what song would that be?

2. If this part of you was a character in a movie what would this movie be about?

3. What kinds of people like to hang out with this character that is a part of you?

4. Would you rather leave your hometown and never be able to return, or stay in your hometown but never be able to leave?

5. How long have you been a part of me in my life?

6. When was the first time you can remember showing up doing what you do?

7. What type of people do you feel most relaxed hanging out with?

8. What are you doing when you feel the most confident?

9. If someone is mean to you what is the best way to be towards them?

10. What is your most embarrassing moment?

11. What do you do when you feel scared?

12. What do you want to do when someone embarasses you?

13. What is something that has happened when you felt shame?

14. What helps you feel safe?

15. What other part of you do you find the most annoying?

16. What do you think could happen if that annoying part just wasn't there any more?

17. What makes it most annoying?

18. If this annoying part was your partner in life how would you relate to it differently?

19. What are you concerned would happen to me if you didn't do the thing you were best at doing?

20. If you could go on vacation and not work so hard for me where would you go and do?

Look over your answers, with this part of you in your awareness. What's the purpose of this part of you right now? How is it trying to help you in your life? Its solution doesn't work for all of you, but you can see it means well.

Write down the good intention of that part.

If you'd like to do this exercise with other parts, there are blank pages at the back of this book you can use.

Exercise Two: Go DEEP to connect and build relationships on the inside

Bodyguards are there to prevent you from feeling emotional hurt. But what specifically are your bodyguards protecting you from?

Now we will go deeper to find out from whom or what your parts are protecting you. To do this, we will go DEEP to become mindful of what is happening inside of you right now. DEEP stands for Discover, Explore, Embrace, and Pinpoint.

If Exercise One helped you to hear from your part, this exercise is about letting answers come to you through your body.

The DEEP exercise is where you begin working more closely with your parts. It's more important than ever to make sure you're in Self before you begin this exercise or the ones that follow.

An easy litmus test for being in Self is to ask, "How do I feel toward this part of me?" If you feel Calm, Curious, and Compassionate toward this part, you're in Self. If you feel aggravated, judgmental, sad, or even extremely enthusiastic, you're blended with, or in a part.

If you're blended with a part, take a few minutes to sit quietly and do some deep breathing to re-center yourself in your body. Then approach your part again and see if it feels different.

Directions

Set yourself up in a quiet place where you will not be interrupted by your cat, dog, or other loved one. Breathe deeply and allow your body to completely relax. It's time to go DEEP.

#1 Discover where you feel this emotion in or around your body

Become mindful of your inner world to **discover** the part of you that wants to write to you. Let your parts know you're interested in hearing their stories, needs, and wants.

Do you have a thought, feeling, or sensation that seems stronger than others?

Maybe at first it feels like stress. You say, "I feel stressy." Let Stressy come forward by noticing it.

Name it as this part steps forward.

#2 Explore this sensation

Focus on Stressy. Fill out this feeling thought or sensation. Bring it into the foreground by noticing it and describing it to yourself.

Describe it to yourself as a physical feeling in your body. Is it a tightness in your jaw or a tingling in your arms or legs?

Describe the part exactly how it shows up. Do you see an image or does a name pop into your head? Maybe even an animal? Do you feel a sick feeling in your stomach or a tightness across your back? If you feel confusion, then write from that. Whatever you feel or sense see it as a part of you giving you information. What does that feel like?

#3 Embrace this part of you

Connect with this part of you in a caring respectful way. In your mind's eye, let this part know you would like to know it better.

Ask it to write down whatever it would like you to know. Let the story come only from this part, no matter what other parts or sides of you might want to say.

Ask any interrupting parts to wait beside you as you hear from this part. Be a friend to this part of you and listen with an open heart. See if you can understand the essence of what this part wants you to know.

If you're not feeling friendly towards your visiting part, your part probably won't open up to you. Instead turn your attention to the part of you that feels judgey and unfriendly.

Be Curious towards it. Ask it if it can step aside so you can get to know the first part. All parts are welcome just not all at once.

Visualize handing this part of you the pen, and asking them and only them to answer these questions.

How are you helping me with how you show up in my body and/or in my life?

What do you like about your role in my life? What do you like about your work? What do you wish you didn't have to do so much?

#4 Pinpoint this part's concerns

Now you want to find out what concerns this part has. Let your Calm, Curious Self ask these questions of your part.

What are you worried will happen if you don't do what you do?

What other parts might get bigger if what you do would get smaller?

As you're telling me your worries, do you feel the presence of Self? Do you feel listened to and appreciated by the larger Self that is you?

Is there a need or want you have right now, that could be met in real time?

Did your Self hear this? Could Self write down how it will meet this need in real time?

Exercise #3: An origin story

Protectors are born out of a need to cope with extreme feelings or emotions from traumatic events that take place early in life. Understanding from whence they came allows us to know them and empathize with them better.

A part's origin story doesn't always have to be traumatic or dramatic, it can be an experience or an accumulation of experiences that occurred in your past that may have caused you emotional pain and then a protector came about.

This exercise will help you identify where, long ago, you placed a bandage over a wound. You won't be removing the bandage in this exercise. You are just finding out where it is, and why it was placed there.

Directions

Give it some thought and write an origin story for one of your parts on the next page. Think about how this part manifests in your adult life and from what it might be trying to protect you.

CHAPTER THREE

DISCOVERING YOUR EXILES

"Weeds are flowers too once you get
to know them."
- A.A. Milne

Now that you've gotten closer to your protectors and they've started to understand and connect more with your Self, it's time to meet your exiled parts. All along your protectors have been shielding you from the difficult feelings and stories trapped inside your exiled parts. These are younger, more vulnerable parts you may not be entirely aware of, because your protectors exiled them from your inner system.

Our **exiles** formed in response to pain and distress during our childhoods.

- They are young and vulnerable

- They've been shut out by your protectors so you don't feel their pain

- They are often burdened with old, outdated beliefs formed during difficult or traumatic times

- They are very sensitive and hold emotional pain

- When they are triggered, they come back strongly into your awareness and you can feel their strong negative emotions (hurt, anger, shame)

- They need the Calm, Compassion, and Curiosity of Self when you meet them, not feelings of anger or judgment

- Getting to know your exiles means feeling their raw, painful emotions. This chapter may be the most difficult for you to work through because exiled parts are so vulnerable.

Karen's Story

To guide you, I want to share a story. A friend of mine - we'll call her Karen - was deeply ashamed of her boisterous, loud laugh. Her classmates made fun of her for it. But more painfully, her mother would block her ears when Karen laughed. So Karen formed a group of parts inside to protect her from embarrassing herself in public. Whenever she imagined people were making fun of her laugh, she'd immediately be flooded with her exile's feelings of shame and the pain of her classmates rejecting her for being "too weird."

I'll reference this story as we go through the exercises in this chapter.

Important note: If the bad feelings get too intense, turn to Chapter Five for the rescue exercise or else consult with a professional counselor. Some exiles may be too hard to work with by yourself.

Exercise One: Meet your exiles

In this exercise you'll meet just one exile at a time. No living rooms full of parts here like in Chapter One. Your exile will write a letter to your Self to introduce itself and share what it needs from you.

Meeting your exiles is different than meeting your protectors. Your protectors are more visible and more present in your life. Your exiles, however, are exiled. They're farther away. When we bring them in close to meet them, we feel their emotions.

So, you'll need to ask your protectors for permission to meet with the exiles they are guarding. (If you don't get their permission, continue to meet with your protectors so they keep growing their trust in Self.)

Maybe in the past, you tried to meet your exiles only to have your protectors rush in to prevent you from feeling the agony they can bring. It will be different this time, however, because your protectors have connected with you in Self energy. There is more trust in your inner system overall.

This time you will bring the Calm, Compassion, and Curiosity of Self when you ask your exiles not to overwhelm you with emotions. You and your Self are right there with them, and they can feel and trust you.

Karen's exile formed when she changed schools in 3rd grade. She had many friends at her old school, but kids at the new school thought she was weird. She felt so lonely and sad as a result. She formed a belief that nobody could ever like her as she was, and her weird laugh proved it.

Over time she developed a protector that kept this young vulnerable part out of her conscious system. This protector made sure she didn't try to make new friends because they might make fun of her.

Directions

Take this opportunity to sit quietly with one of your young vulnerable parts that feels sad, lonely, scared, or ashamed. Maybe it is hanging around because of something happening right now in your life. Here is your chance to be with it as you would be with a good friend.

First let's get permission from the protector you talked to in Exercise Two in the previous chapter. You used DEEP to learn what this protector is protecting you from.

I recommend following the ground rules in the "Opening the lines of communication at the meeting place" exercise on page 12.

This next conversation must be Self-led. If you find that you're not in Self when you start the exercise, go back to the Meeting Place exercise to hear from your parts.

Find this part in you now. Sense it, imagine it, and feel it in or around you right now.

Ask: how do you feel about this vulnerable part (exile) of you? If you feel any of the "C" qualities of Self (Calm, Compassion, Curiosity, Courage, Creativity, Connection, Confidence, Clarity), you're good to go. Your Self is present to witness.

Let this part of you show you its story of how it got this way. Here are some questions to guide you.

How old are you?

Where do you live in my body? Where do I sense you when you show up?

What are your concerns if you show up in everyday life?

What beliefs do you hold about life?

What burdens are you carrying from those difficult younger times?

How long have you been a part of me?

Can you remember the first time you felt how you did?

What was happening?

Are you aware that you are not alone and that I am here with you?

You are a part of me now. I was not able to be with you when you were a small child and hurting. Tell me about your hurts.

What are your concerns if you show up in everyday life?

The letter

Now it's time to write your letter telling the story of what happened long ago that hurt you emotionally.

Tell your story from this young part that your system exiled out so it would not have to feel its pain. Witness this story from your larger adult Self.

Just write freely without worrying about spelling or punctuation for now. Write for 5-10 minutes, and at the end, write what you feel you desire from your Self.

After you have written the letter, sit quietly in your Self qualities and read the letter. Reflect on what you've learned before responding to this exiled part of you. You may even want to write a letter from Self back to your vulnerable part, letting it know you heard from it and you care.

Begin your letter here.

Exercise Two: Give your exiles an update

Believe it or not, your vulnerable parts may be unaware of who you are right now. They don't know how old you are or where you live. This lack of knowledge is one reason they are so afraid. They are not connected with your larger adult Self. They have been shut out and in exile. Now is the opportunity to bring them into your present day life.

Directions

Write this part a letter to tell them who you are as your adult Self now. Answer these questions:

- What do you do for work?

- Do you have a family?

- What are your accomplishments?

- How have things changed in the years since they were born?

- What do you love to do?

Explain or show them how their old, outdated beliefs can change. They are not all true now. See where holding this belief has limited you in your everyday life. Understand this belief was from a long ago time when you were young and not able to meet your needs.

Karen gently shared with her exile that her friends, co-workers, and even her mother liked her laugh now!

They told her it made them laugh more and they were proud when they said something funny that made her laugh. Because her exile felt the calming reassurance of Self, she felt her exile start to relax.

Is there a need that you could take care of in the present for yourself so that you do not live out this belief as if it were true?

For example, you may have a belief your emotions are not as important as other people's. Tell this younger part of you that you will feel your emotions and not deny them now. Reassure your exile you will not leave, but instead defend your emotions by trying to meet the need in the moment.

Your letter should start with something like, *"This was really hard when you were little. I am so sorry this happened to you. You are with me now and not alone. You don't have to be there in that time and that story any more. You are a part of me and so much more has happened in your life. Come out of that story in that time long ago and stay with me now. Let me tell you a little about us now."*

Begin your letter here.

Exercise Three: Letting go, the unburdening

In IFS we describe exiles as being burdened. We can let go of these burdens and beliefs when they are seen by the larger Self. The exiled parts are burdened with their beliefs from an earlier time and the feelings that accompany those beliefs.

Exiles are like children, and can possess many of the same qualities that children do. Exiles can be curious, spontaneous, playful, and imaginative. Burdened exiles have no room, however, for any of these qualities. The burden is too big.

Getting to know an exile and helping it heal by witnessing its stories gives the exile the opportunity to let this belief and heavy burden go. When this happens it feels lighter. Now there is room for those other qualities. So we invite them in to us.

Karen felt her caring Self witness her exile's pain as she wrote about it. The love and connection she felt on the inside changed her relationship to this hurting part. For the first time, the exiled part could believe people liked her laugh and also her. Once the exile let go of its burden, it felt more playful and joyful. The protector who made her avoid groups relaxed, and was able to join other parts that scanned for social safety.

Directions

Write in more detail about the event or events that caused this exile to form. You may need to spend some time listening and hearing from this part as they tell you how it was for them. Often there were many incidents during your childhood that happened that fed this belief and these will come to you. This information could come to you over many days or even in your dreams. Write it down as it comes to you. It helps to write it down because writing supports this part to stay *separate* from you as you listen and reflect back your caring and concern. Be the writer and the observer in Self.

Begin writing here.

What happened to give you the beliefs you wrote down in Exercise One? Was there some extreme difficulty, a form of neglect and/or abuse? Even not being seen or cared for by good parents can be traumatic and burden us for years to come.

What belief does this part continue to hold onto from that experience? For example, perhaps changing schools and not having good friends made this part believe that it wasn't good enough, unworthy or too different to fit in.

Did your exile feel connection inside with Self? A sign of connection is the exile being able to share its pain *without* flooding your entire system with its emotions. This is because the exile felt all of the "C" qualities of Self. Don't be surprised if this exile part doesn't feel quite finished even if it feels like it gave up its burden and beliefs. There may be other stories it will want to share with you at another time. But you can give up some of the burden now.

Reflect briefly on how it was for you doing this exercise.

Now that your exile feels connected on the inside with Self, you can gently inquire whether or not the exile feels ready to let go of any or all of their old beliefs. Refer to your work in Exercise Two to help your exile see that many things really have changed, and they can let go of those old beliefs that aren't true anymore. Remind them they are not alone now. They are connected to you.

Gently inquire of this part, are you ready to let go of any or all of your old beliefs?

Optional Exercise: A symbolic unburdening

Some of my clients have found it helpful to perform a ceremony to symbolize letting go of their exile's burden. A ceremony or symbolic act can help bring your exiled part back into the family system and let it know it will be looked after in a loving way.

Feeling encouraged by her Self connection, Karen told her mother about the pain she'd felt when she would put her fingers in her ears when Karen laughed. Karen was able to heal from the outside, too. Later Karen's mother gave her a framed picture of a woman laughing with the words "Keep being the one with the crazy laugh!" Karen proudly displays this in her home as a symbol of embracing who she is.

Directions

One suggestion for a symbolic act is to write the burden down on a piece of paper and dispose of it through one of the four elements: Wind, Fire, Earth, or Water. For example, you could write it down on a piece of paper and then burn it.

Or you could borrow from the Jewish custom of Tashlich which means "casting off" in Hebrew and involves symbolically casting off the sins of the previous year (or in this case, your exile's burden) by tossing pieces of bread or another food into a body of flowing water.

Once you've completed your symbolic unburdening, record here what you did. It can be as simple as writing the date and time or as elaborate as cutting and pasting in a photo.

Enter what feels right for you.

The results you'll get from this exercise will play out over time, not immediately. It takes time for the effects of a ceremony to take root. Look for signs as the days pass.

Exercise Four: Imagine the future

What will life be like, now that your exile has let go of its burden, and your protectors don't need to work so hard anymore? Take some time to appreciate your new freedom. Write it down so you can learn from the experience.

Directions

List the qualities or gifts that this young part will have the opportunity to experience now that it is free of the burdens it once held. Playfulness? Generosity? Dancing? Connecting with others?

What will your life look like now that you have more of these qualities?

Check in with your protectors: they no longer need to watch over this exiled part of you. They have *new* jobs in your life! What are they? They could even go on vacation. What do you feel excited to do? More ideas may come to you over time. Be sure to revisit this page to write them down.

You want to reinforce this new way of being in the world. Write down how Self will make time to meet daily with this young part to build on this new and fragile connection.

CHAPTER FOUR

MOVING FORWARD

"I own my fantasies, my dreams, my hopes, my fears.
I own all my triumphs and successes, all my failures
and mistakes. Because I own all of me, I can become
intimately acquainted with me. By so doing I can
love me and be friendly with me in all my parts."

— Virginia Satir, "My Declaration of Self-Esteem"
(1975)

Every experience has a beginning, middle, and end. Your experience of
writing in this workbook and getting to know your parts is coming to a
close.

As you turn toward the future, it's important to understand these new
connections inside are fragile and will need your attention and care to
grow strong. Nurture your inner bonds with your Self qualities.

Because of the personal development work you've done, your extreme
parts may need to find new jobs. They no longer need to act as
bodyguards for your exiled parts. Your exiles are now better connected
to your Self and are becoming a part of your inner family system.

**The most important thing to remember is: this is a practice, not
a perfect.** Getting more Self, nurturing those inner connections,
responding from Self rather than reacting to a part? It will be ongoing
and interactive. You will be learning, not performing. So don't try to be
perfect about it. Give yourself permission to *practice* instead of trying
to *perform* a new skill. Take a deep breath - you have the support of
your Self to lean on.

Exercise One: Mapping your new "what is"

Now is a good time to assess what I call the *what is*.
As I've written on my blog:

> There will be no real change in our lives until **we can see our situation and accept it**. To accept it does not mean that we are agreeing that it will stay that way forever although that might be our fear.

Your situation, exactly as it is, is your *what is*. It's your reality. In this exercise you'll map your new what is.

In this exercise, you'll check in with your usual suspects to find out how they are feeling in light of all this Self discovery. In doing this writing and personal growth you have transformed or updated old beliefs about yourself and let go of old stories. This means that you are relating differently on the inside: there are different relationships and inner bonds that have formed.

Directions

Cultivate more Self inside of you by sitting in stillness and attending to your breath. Breathe deeply and exhale out longer then inhaling. Sense the Calm that gets activated when you spend time doing this activity. Invite yourself to feel the excitement of the unknown and feel Courage too. Wonder how you will be Creative in this new place.

Notice what still feels familiar about your personality. What are the parts of yourself that manage and run your everyday life? List them here.

Are any of them less extreme now that you have gotten to know them and what they want for you?

If some feel extreme still let them know you want to spend more time getting to know them better. By now you will recognize them by the feelings in your body, your thoughts, and/or sensations.

List 3-5 ways you can and intend to pay attention to them in your everyday current life.

Notice and list what feels changed or different in you from your Self exploration. Which parts of you feel different? List them. If they've discovered a new role to play in your life now, write that down too. An example might be if an angry part of you that used to push people away, now has a new role setting boundaries and saying "no thank you."

Now let's talk about what you've learned about your protecting parts.

What have you learned to help you recognize that a part of you has become extreme?

When you notice this part has become extreme, what will you do to be better connected with it either in real time or soon after?

Some of your protectors may have new roles, and some of them may not. For the protectors who haven't found new roles, how might their roles transform now that your vulnerable (formerly exiled) parts are being taken care of by you in Self qualities?

And now, some questions about what you've learned about the vulnerable (exiled) parts you've brought into your inner system.

How do they feel connected to you right now or how do you sense those parts are present with you and part of your inner system?

Describe the part(s) of you that feel vulnerable and young but have updated their beliefs about you.

How do they feel different?

Where do you notice they are in your body?

If they have a new updated view of life what is it?

Now, let's bring it back to all of your parts.

How can you promise to stay present with these newly formed bonds and ways of relating to your inner world?

Examples would be:

- I will ask myself every morning who is there and what requests for the day are present.

- I can write from extreme parts of myself that get triggered by life's events before speaking. After writing from my parts and knowing their need/my need I will speak for that part not from it.

- Every night I will check in with any new relationships I have with my inner parts and see what they need to say to me.

Reflect on what behaviors you could have in your life right now that would support you staying connected to your inner world of parts.

Exercise Two: Take a time machine into the future

What will your life be like now that you are intentionally cultivating your Self qualities? You can either do this exercise by looking across all your parts, or working with a protector part that's feeling more relaxed after the work in the previous chapters.

Directions

Write about what your life will be like now that one of your exiled parts has been unburdened. Just write in stream of consciousness, visualizing the positive changes to come. Bring in your Courage to step out of being cautious.

Describe how your life will be different in one week, one month, and also one year from today.

Exercise Three: Bring your inner world into harmony by cultivating your Self qualities

Paying attention to Self qualities and cultivating this abundant Self in us is also important. Look at your everyday life and see the ways you now are fostering the qualities of Self: Calm, Compassion, Curiosity, Courage, Creativity, Connection, Confidence, and Clarity.

We have an abundance of these Self qualities. When we sense these qualities within and lead with them in our everyday life we actually feel connected and at our best. We make the best choices for ourselves. We create a life that fits us and supports us. Set the intention to incorporate activities, interactions, and thoughts that would promote the flow of more Self within and without.

Directions

What are some ways you can cultivate the C's? List your own ways here. I've put some ideas in to spur your Creativity.

Calm
Rest, meditate, take time for stillness, be sure to breathe deeply at all those red lights

Compassion

Be your own best friend, tell yourself: I am so proud you got up early (for example)

Curiosity

Wonder about: yourself and others, fixed ideas you hold, sensations in your body

Courage

Experiment with stepping up to things that feel hard, fake it until you make it

Creativity

Sing in the shower, tell a story, cook, bake, garden, dance, do laughter yoga

Connection

Connect inside with play, connect with someone else who needs what you can offer

Confidence

Decide to decide and see what happens, start with small things and go bigger

Clarity

Stand in a place of knowing, reflect on what you already feel clear about and name it. Help mentor someone who's more of a beginner than you

Exercise Four: Your new rescue exercise

While you were doing this work, I encouraged you to read Chapter Five anytime it felt too hard. Now you've completed this work, this is your new rescue exercise.

As you move forward in life, don't be surprised when your parts get extreme from time to time. It can still happen. Situations like these can trigger extreme reactions:

- Transitions in life

- Times of hardship

- Times of uncertainty

- Relating during conflicts

- Managing extreme worries or fears about the future

As you've learned so far, it's important to have a talk with the protector part that has gotten too big. Usually, you can't do this in the heat of the moment. Later, when you're alone, that's when you can have this conversation.

Directions

Go inside and sense the emotions, thoughts, feelings, or sensations your extreme protector is sending to you. Have a dialogue with this part from a Self-led place.

1. Ask the activated part that is protecting you right now, "What are you concerned will happen if you take action about your current situation?"

2. Ask the protector, "How is this situation different than in the past?" Gently remind this part of you how things have changed, much like you did in Chapter Three.

3. Take time to appreciate this part for how it protected you in the past. Let it know you are mature and grown up now. People won't hurt you the same as when you were little. Thank this part for taking care of you before you became the person you are now. You know it helped you survive some things. Now is now and is different from the past.

4. Write a letter from Self to the protecting part. This is where you bring everything together to help soothe this part.

- State the concern of this protector as you understand it.

- Let the protector know you noticed how it's been trying to help you, and send Compassion, Appreciation and Gratitude for how hard this part is working for you right now.

- Show your protector how you hear what it advises and if there's something you can do in real time with this advice, explain how you will do so.

- Conclude by explaining why its fears will not come true this time.

Ask this part to withdraw and step back and not take the lead in this decision around this current topic. Welcome it to advise you of its concerns but not to take over.

CHAPTER FIVE
RESCUE CHAPTER

"I listen with love to my inner voice."
— Louise Hay

Using this book is hard work. Learning about yourself, and healing yourself from past emotional hurts, is hard work. You can expect difficult emotions to come up.

In the past, when you found yourself flooded with sadness, anger, stress, or fear, you've probably turned to eating, drinking alcohol, shopping, or surfing the TV or internet to cope.

These activities have something in common:

- They bring quick relief

- The relief is fleeting

- You actually feel worse later on

Please, don't engage in those bandage behaviors. Instead, read this rescue chapter first and see if it helps.

The best part is you can come back to this way of journaling from your parts as many times as you like with different parts of yourself. But, the more work you do in this workbook, the less often you'll need this chapter - or the bandages.

Important: When you turn towards a loud part within, you may feel worse before you feel better. That's because this part wants to be known by your larger Self - emotional pain and all.

You're finally connecting with this loud part, and it has a lot to say. When you stay with it and feel it, you get better connected with yourself. You know yourself better.

In the past, getting closer may have meant being completely hijacked by a loud part. You can connect and stay separate from emotionally strong parts of yourself by being Curious toward these parts. Say to this part, "I didn't know it felt THIS bad. What's going on, that you feel this bad?" That noticing and responding keeps you separate from your big emotions. You are not just this big emotion. You are also Self, interested and curious.

> If feeling worse turns into an emotional crisis, please seek help from good friends or a professional counselor immediately. You may not be able to do this work alone, and that's okay. If you can't get a hold of someone urgently, go to the emergency department of the nearest hospital.

Exercise: Take a Self care timeout

For this exercise, the first step is to notice that you feel extreme, and then let that extreme part write down everything it's thinking and feeling.

It's important not to judge or critique this part, especially if you disagree with it. The part needs to write *its* truth, not *the* truth. Let it say, "nobody loves me" or "I am a selfish person who hurts everyone" even if another part of you wants to step in to correct it. Just let it write.

Directions

First, what feeling do you notice? Or maybe you notice a thought instead. Maybe you notice that you desperately want to head to the nearest pub, or hit up the ice cream shop.

The thought that pops into your head might be, "I really need to rest on the sofa and watch TV all night eating my favorite fast foods. Or, "After a day like this, I deserve to head to <name of your favorite store> and buy <this or that>."

Write down the extreme feelings, thoughts, or beliefs popping up right now for you.

"I am so tired" and "that makes me sad too" for example.

Be curious toward this part of you that holds this big feeling. View it as a part of you that holds information, that's all. Your part wants to share that information with you.

As you write, direct this part to open up to you by asking questions like:

- What does it feel like?

- What are you telling yourself when you have this feeling?

- What's happening right now that you feel the need to be so large or extreme right now?

You have just met a part of you in the above exercise. You could have even given it a name or maybe it named itself. Now, give this part an opportunity to let it all out. Write from it. Let that part take control of your pen and say what it needs to say. There is no thinking involved here just the part letting you know what it needs you to know.

Important: Set the intention to write with your heart open and feel your Compassion toward this hurting part of you that is writing.

Be gentle with this part that is also you. Say to yourself, "I know it's so hard right now" and "I know you feel <sad, angry, hurt, confused>. What do you need or want from me to help?"

When you finish writing take a minute to be quiet with yourself. Breathe deeply, feeling where the Calm is in your body. Notice how you feel different than when you started and where you feel the same.

At this point you can either read what you wrote, or set it aside and take a break.

If you *are* ready to read what you just wrote, imagine you're listening to a good friend tell you how they are hurting. Give yourself the same friendliness and caring toward what you're reading.

If you're *not* ready, put it aside and practice some Self care to bring Calm to your inner system.

- Take a walk in nature

- Go for a run or swim

- Visit with friends

- Do a Self Compassion exercise [1]

- Do some Yoga Nidra meditations [2]

There's no need to run through this. Take your time and notice all that's going on inside of you without judging or trying to figure it out. After you have taken a rest go back and read what you wrote with Compassion and non-judgment. It is so hard for you right now this makes sense you would feel this way too.

Remember: This is just how it is for now, soon this too will change, and something else will come into your awareness.

[1] Visit my website for a free Self Compassion exercise: **http://bit.ly/selfcom**
[2] Visit my website to download a free Yoga Nidra meditation:
http://bit.ly/yoganid16

CONCLUSION

"All know that the drop merges into the ocean. But few know that the ocean merges into the drop."

— Kabir, 15th-century Indian poet

Let's take a moment to reflect on what you've accomplished in your journey to meet your parts.

Getting to know your parts is hard work. Connecting with them means feeling all of their raw emotions from when they were burdened with their painful beliefs from long ago.

You had to use all eight qualities of Self to go inside and meet them: Calm, Compassion, Curiosity, Courage, Creativity, Connection, Confidence, and Clarity. Be proud of yourself! Don't just pat yourself on the back, give yourself a big hug.

My hope is that as you let your parts feel your healing Self energy shine through, they began to relax from their extreme roles and trust your Self to lead.

As your Self becomes more in charge, difficulties that arise in your life will be easier to manage. Your new inner awareness means you'll understand when a part of you is in an extreme reaction, and you can step back into Self leadership and steer out of the chaos.

This Self has the essence of an inner mentor, loving parent, and number one fan. The answers are inside you. The exercises you've completed here have taught you how to separate from your parts, get more access to Self and then meet your parts so you can treat them as advisors and not leaders. Speak for them when needed and not from them. At any time you can come back to the exercises in this book to help you connect with more Self.

As you go about interacting in your day and relating to others you will see yourself showing up with these Self qualities in real time. Not just inside with your parts but also in your external world. Your outside relationships will positively change as you bring Self qualities into connection with others, too.

Maintaining your new-found inner harmony means staying friendly and Curious with your protectors and newly found young (previously exiled) parts. Check in with them each day. You'll feel the weight lift off your heart as you continue to foster connection with your exiled parts in particular. Let all your parts know you are there with your Calm, Compassion, and Connecting Self to guide the way.

ACKNOWLEDGMENTS

Many passionate, dedicated teachers influenced the thinking and ideas in this book. I owe a large debt to Richard C. Schwartz, PhD, the innovator of the IFS therapeutic model, and many of my IFS colleagues who have taught and written extensively about the subject.

I am grateful to Toni Herbine-Blank and Nancy Sowell, IFS practitioners who have guided and supported me through my IFS career. Both of you have at times pushed me, challenged me, and also brought forth strength I didn't know I had.

A big thank you to my publishing team at Moondog Marketing & Media. I especially want to thank my editor Jenn Whinnem, whose Self dances with mine in creativity, connection, and collaboration. And a big thank you to Juanjo Montilla, Chief Creative Officer, for bringing the book to visual life.

Thank you to my late friend leslie wanner who was always my "number one fan" when she was alive. She lived her life in generosity and love.

I never could have gotten here without the love and support of my family. Many thanks to my parents for their gifts of a positive life perspective (that's you, Dad) and believing in me, which taught me to believe in myself (thanks, Mom). To my husband, Peter, thank you for holding together the loving and and not always calm container of family life. And last but not least, a big thank you to my loving children: Maribeth, for pushing me along as she pulled this idea out of me and into that first Word document; Rebecca, for being my workshop partner and polishing my ideas; and Nick and Tor who encourage and inspire me by the Self-led way they live their lives.

And to all of my clients over the years: your courage gave me courage. Thank you for the role you've played in my life.

Notes to Self

Notes to Self

Notes to Self

Notes to Self

Notes to Self

Notes to Self

Made in the USA
Lexington, KY
19 August 2019